Allrite, My Sun

Nah El Publications

Soul Rhymer Productions

Published by Nah El Publications
1255 Race Track Road
Sumter, S.C. 29153

Cover design by Neterankhhotep-El for Soul Rhymer
Productions

Portion One – The Introduction

I'm different. I think different. I act different. When you have an overstanding (a better substitute for the word, "understanding") of how life operates, you can begin to make your own rules and laws.

I flow, I spit, I rhyme. Whatever you like to call it. I'm nice with it; I'm cold with it. It's just a hobby and I feel like if I really had dedicated my life to the craft that I would be through the roof with it.

Anyway, when most people started their verses off they began with the "Yo, Yo." If you don't overstand what I'm talking about then you're probably too young. Wait a minute, you are young. Well listen up youngin'. Like I was saying, a lot of people started their verses with the ad lib of "Yo, Yo." That was the warm up, the double dutch of "I'm about to jump in and begin spitting my rhymes." I don't know how or when it started but I begin saying "Allrite." That was my introduction, that was my warm up, that was my ad lib to let people know that I was about to jump in.

It's a reason why I spell Allrite this way. The main reason is because I want to. Now I could have spelled it All Right or Alright but which of these would be right?

Alright has been in use almost as long as All Right. You have different people who swear by the spelling of one over the other. I'm a poet and a writer so I overstand how the world of spelling words operates, therefore I make my own rules and laws.

For the purpose of this book, I will use my way of spelling Allrite. My reasoning behind this will be seen in this quick break down.

Allrite
All + rite
Rite = Rites of Passage
Rites = Rituals

This book is a guideline. This book is a manual. This book will teach you rituals to learn. Don't be spooked by the word ritual. Ritual just means an act or acts that you do the same way over and over to accomplish something. Brushing your teeth is a ritual because you do the same thing over and over every morning to accomplish something, maintaining good teeth.

Learning these rituals within this book is going to be your rites of passage. Rites of passage are rituals that you will be performing to take you from being a boy to pass you over to becoming a man. Are you ready? Let's go.

Portion Two – So You're A Man Now Huh?

You're a teenager now right? You have the world all figured out right? I'm here to tell you that you may as well sit down or take a knee. Listen son. The game is all twisted. The world isn't exactly what you may have believe it to be. Let me tell you why.

First of all, let me ask you this, "What have your father taught you?" See, a lot of us grew up in homes without a father or maybe our father was in the home but didn't teach us much. So what happens? The streets teach us, T.V. teaches us and the radio teaches us.

I'm going to be straight up with you son. And when I say son, don't get frustrated by it and think I'm trying to belittle you. Like Method Man said in a rap song, "I call you son/sun because you shine like one!"

On the real son, keeping it a buck with you, I'm not the man I thought I'd be. Where I'm at right now as I'm typing and putting this book together...I never pictured this. I'm supposed to be married with about 7 children right now. I said 7 but ask around, I always said 20, to keep it a hundred. Anyway, I always seen myself as a family man and being with the mother of my children. It might not be in the stars for that one.

I tell you what though, that's the purpose of this book. If I'm not there physically for my son…for my sons and even daughters, I want them to know that I am with them spiritually and mentally. This book is my voice. Read it. Listen to these words. This is my last attempt, my last resort to be a part of their lives and YOUR life.

I want to drop jewels for you. Here is my way of providing some type of guidance and wisdom. The seed of greatness is in you. That Divine light is within. I'm just a spark, you all will be the flame!

Portion Three – Number One

Rule Number one is about Number One, meaning yourself. You must take care of yourself first. There's a saying that, "You cannot pour from an empty cup." You must gain knowledge of self. That means you must learn who you are from a historical stand point, culturally and biologically.

Learning your history and where you came from along with the culture your people belong to or practiced is very important. Knowing who you are is of the utmost importance because it is then you have something to measure everything else against.

From race, color, ethnicity or nationality, everybody's not the same. So with that in mind, our body requirements and make up is different. Those of us who have subscribed to the label as African American or Black, requires different types of food compared to non-African American or non-Blacks.

What we eat affects the way our body behaves. What we eat also affects the way our mind operates. Remember I told you Rule Number One is about Self. Taking care of numeral uno. If you can't take care of yourself then you'll be in no position to help anyone else. If you're sick, how can you help another person fix a car or build a house?

This is why we must eat right to maintain a strong body and sound mind. I am a vegan. That means I do not eat any animals including fish. I do not drink any milk from any animals. I do not eat the eggs of any animals. And I do not eat cheese or any other product that is made with animal ingredients.

There will be many people who oppose the life of a vegan. These same people say that we need different animals or animal by product for a healthy life. They mention different things like protein but cannot explain to you what protein is. They speak of nutrients but these are the same people who use microwave ovens to heat up or cook food and at the same time kill all the nutrients in the food.

They don't tell you the facts that man have survived for millions of years without eating animals. They don't tell you that our bodies aren't designed to process meat. Natural meat eaters have short intestines. Humans have long intestines. Meat eaters have sharp teeth to rip through the flesh of its prey. Humans use forks and knives.

If eating meat was natural for humans we could go out into the wild right now and have a meal. But humans, in order for us to eat meat, what must be done? We have to catch it, clean it, season it and then cook it. But how long have stoves been in homes? Those who is in opposition of veganism don't tell you that even the F.D.A. has admitted that meat is causing cancer.

The things we call food now is killing us under the name of cancer, diabetes, high blood pressure and other illnesses. How can we be efficient in doing the first most important thing, taking care of Self, if we are not careful in choosing the correct food to consume?

This is what I'm telling you. We must minimize the amount of processed food and meat that we consume IF we choose to consume these things. It would be best to cut it out altogether. This is one of the tasks that I present to you. You must carry and fulfil this duty. Eat as close to a vegan or vegetarian diet. This is part of your culture. We live in a fast food world, do not succumb to it. It has gotten to the point where the food in the grocery stores are not as nutritional as they should be.

Grow a garden. Farm some land. This is how we overcome this little situation that we are facing when it comes to good food. Good food leads to a strong body and a sound mind. This generation that is under me has become lazy. Not only the generation under me but my generation too.

We are no longer active in the physical sense. Children do not run and play outside anymore. Everyone's stuck in the house watching T.V. and playing video games. Oh how I would love to spend my days outside. I sacrifice most my opportunity to do so, as I am preparing my children for a better life. I used to be confined by the walls of plantations which the majority of people call jobs or work.

I'm now sacrificing my time to build something for you. I'm here to give you a guideline so that you can think outside the box. You don't need a job. Why have a job when you can run your own business? This is the mindset I want to instill in my children. You don't have to be an employee; you can be the boss!

But first, let me get back to my point about being outside. We have to become active again. When I say, "We" I really mean, "You." This is part of your rites of passage. We have to get back into exercising and staying fit. Being in shape is important and of course, you see how it ties back into Number One, taking care of Self. There are many forms of exercises that we can do. You don't have to be an athlete to be healthy. Just exercise on the regular.

You'd be surprise of the number of people who can't even stand outside in the sun for a few minutes without complaining. Just imagine these type of people trying to be active outdoors. Getting some sun on our skin is very important. Not everybody has sun friendly skin. Melanoma and other skin cancers are high in non melanated (Black) peoples.

Long walks in the sun is a starting point. If you don't want to spend all your time lifting weights or doing strenuous exercises; walking, jogging and running are very good. Bike riding is a favorite of mine also. I love riding my bike on country roads while enjoying different sights. It's amazing how the same road you travel on in a car may appear totally different while riding a bike.

Other forms of exercises that you may enjoy are yoga and martial arts. Yoga is very good as it teaches you different poses which allows the body to stretch as it loosens tight muscles and ligaments while allowing the energy in the body to flow more freely.

I was always fascinated by martial arts and wanted to take up some classes. I never received the chance to as a child but my love for it never died. I love watching "karate movies" as I call them.

My two favorite styles of martial arts are Capoeira and Muy Thai. I would love to combine those two. Capoeira to me seems like a graceful and peaceful form. It incorporates the entire body and the upper body has to be just as strong as the lower body, if not stronger.

Capoeira is a smooth, rhythmic, dance art. Muy Thai seems to be its complete opposite, in my eyes that is. Muy Thai is fiercer. With hard blows using the elbows and knees, Muy Thai is unleashing all your anger through your strikes. Of course those who teach this form of martial arts will completely disagree, I'm speaking from my perspective and the best way I can describe it.

Taking up martial arts, yoga, lifting weights, bike riding or just walking being active outside, teaches us discipline on many levels. I know I mentioned not too long ago that Muy Thai is like unleashing all your anger through your strikes but Muy Thai along with all other forms of martial arts teaches you how to control your anger and other emotions.

You must be disciplined when taking on an opponent. Letting your emotions over power your logic and training can lead to serious trouble. Not being disciplined can lead you to striking too hard or not the intended target.

You have to be disciplined when lifting weights because going too fast or attempting to lift more than you're actually ready for can cause serious bodily harm or even death.

Even in bike riding you have to be disciplined because you have to know how far you can actually ride the bike before your legs may cramp up and you need to be disciplined to remind yourself that you need to stay hydrated in activities such as these.

Discipline is all about learning yourself and training your mind. If you have a disciplined mind you can achieve many things. A disciplined mind is a sound mind. That means you have trained your mind to focus and work in your favor.

Portion Four – Gifts

At a young age, embrace what brings you joy. You were born into this world with a gift. Some people may see that particular gift that you were born with and try to cultivate it for you. They will assist you in bringing that gift to fruition. They are here to help you manifest that gift so the rest of the world can see it.

Many of us are not aware of the gift we possess and it may take our entire lives before we recognize it. For those of us who are not so lucky to know or have others around who can see it in us, we can develop talents, skills and trades. These things are of great importance and will help us in the future.

Acquiring skills and having a trade will give us a stepping stone in the future for being independent. With certain skills and trades we will become self-sustained and learn how to be an entrepreneur.

As a child, my father taught me how to change the oil in a car. As an adult, I'm able to change the oil in my car and I can even change oil in other people's car that do not know how to and then charge them money. I wasn't born knowing how to change oil but I was shown and it was a skill that I acquired.

Just from learning how to change the oil in a car led me to being able to do other minor things on a car. By no means am I a mechanic but I can do some things without being dependent on another person.

How would you feel if you were riding in your car and your tire blew out? Do you even know how to change a flat tire and put on a spare? What if you were riding in your car while listening to your favorite artist with the music blasting and all of a sudden the amp stops working, would you know how to fix it? Would you know how to replace the fuse in it or check for loose wires? Or would you have to take it to someone and have them charge you a lot of money to look at it?

I'm using these examples with a car but the same can be applied to your home. What if the refrigerator stops working, how will you keep your food cold? What if a light doesn't turn on when you flip the switch?

Of course we will not be able to fix everything that is broken but what I am suggesting to you is to be knowledgeable in some fields, acquire some skills or trade so that you will be able to handle certain situations when they occur.

Learn the basics of as many things as you can and hopefully you will be a master in one field. Shelter, water and food are the essentials. Learn how to fix things around the house. Learn how to repair water and waste lines. Every man should have a toolbox. Put a hammer in your hand and build something.

Do not wait until a problem arise, practice now so when a problem does occur, you won't be filled with anxiety or nervousness. You will be ready because you've been anticipating this moment.

Let me help you see it another way. Say for instance you needed a couch but didn't have any money. Now there's a man next door selling a couch that has a problem with his truck. You tell the man that you are willing to look at his truck and see if you can fix it for the couch in exchange. He agrees and when you begin to check his truck you find out the starter is bad and replaces it for him. What just took place is called the barter system. The two of you just exchanged goods and services without the need of money.

This is why acquiring skills and trades are important. I know I have been talking about skills and trades but the name of this portion is gifts. Skills and trades can be gifts but let's speak about some gifts that we may have been born with.

Is there anything that you can do very well that no one has taught you how to do? Is there something that you may have even taught yourself how to do very well? One of my gifts is writing. Now I may not write the same as an English professor, but nevertheless I am still a great writer. I have an overstanding when it comes to writing so I'm able to rewrite the rules.

The area of writing that I'm great in is the artistic side of writing. Being that it's an artistic side, I'm able to express myself more freely and not be confined to certain rules that others are bound to. I started out as a poet and when it comes to poetry it takes on so many styles that no one can box me in and say it has to be a certain way.

After some time, I ventured into writing rap lyrics and songs. Rap is an expression of culture. The culture we as black men and women participate in. Rap uses the language of the culture and the black youth which dominates the art, uses a lot of slang. Slang is different words or phrases that's not normally found in the formal context of speaking or writing.

You don't have to spell words correctly as it is written in a dictionary. This is what I mean by my writing being more so of the artistic side. I'm not bound to having to have my words spelled correctly unless I'm writing a book like I'm doing so now.

The gift you are born with can transform your life. It can help move your life in the direction you want it to go. Your gift can also reward you financially. Imagine getting paid for doing what you love to do. Your entire life can be centered around your gift and not the other way around as to only doing what you love as a hobby every once in a while.

Determine what gift you possess and use it. If you're not sure of your gift, ask others about it. Sometimes other people see things in us that we ourselves do not. If you're not sure about your gift, remember that you can always develop skills, talents and trades.

Portion Five – Family

We live in a time now where family values and families all together has been on a decline. I always wanted a big family. You know, me, the wife and all the children. I always wanted a lot of children. It was only my brother and I growing up and later in life we drifted apart. That may just be the reason why I wanted many children.

I never imagined being involved with a woman with a child or children. In a way I guess the Universe was preparing me for that because almost every woman I met had a child or was with child at the moment.

Let me just say my son, that family is very important. I don't care what organization or group you may join, if they don't teach of the importance of family, then you don't need to be a part of it.

Find you a righteous woman. That means a woman who has a pure soul and is concerned with bettering herself, her man and her children. There are so many women out there that is lost that do not know who they are. These women are only concerned with worldly matters; fame, money and looks. Stay away from these kind. They are not suited to be wife although we all can be taught and later change our ways. If you have the chance to teach them, then do so. Let these women know that a lot is depending on them.

By you being a man with knowledge of self, you will be able to pass on knowledge to others. Remember, your first priority is to make sure you know who you are and for you to be a man of substance.

You are thinking right, you are eating right and you are living right. You are preparing yourself to be a family man and a man that will provide for his family and lead his family in the right direction.

Your mission then is to find a suitable mate, a wife or a queen, however you may title her. Let her be of one accord with you. You both must be on the same page. If you meet her and she has no knowledge of self and of culture or history, teach her.

Maintaining a relationship where the man and woman are holding on to different beliefs and values is nearly impossible. You want a healthy relationship where you can enjoy each other, laugh together, learn together and raise your children together properly.

Do not be fooled or tempted by looks only. Looks will fade away. You want someone who will stimulate your mind and touch your heart. You want someone who will have your back and be there for you whenever you need them. The two of you should be a power couple and represent each other well. Spending time with friends and outside family is okay but if you are a family man, your first obligation is to your family. We need more solid families.

If by chance you meet a woman and she has children but there is a connection between the two of you, it is okay to wife her if she is on the same page with you. Do not turn her away because she may be a blessing to you. Of course we would like to have that one woman that no man has touched or share a seed with but many of us are lost without guidance so this is what we must face in today's world.

It is best to begin any journey with just you and the woman. It is at this time that you can get to know each other better and spend large amounts of time together. If this is not an option, like I said before, a woman with a child is fine, as long as the two of you are on the same page or she is willing to learn.

Do not be deceived by these women that may be in it to use you. They may tell you everything that you want to hear just as an unrighteous man would try and trick a woman to use her. Take your time and get to know her. Do this when you are young so you won't feel as if you have to rush everything.

I wish someone was there to teach me this information as a young man but here I am giving this information to you. Maybe that was the reason for me missing the information, so that later in life I could provide it not only for my son but other sons out there in the world. The main thing I want you to remember is that family matters.

Let's build back up our immediate families and then we can reach outward to our communities. Keep a strong and solid family. There will be times when families have issues but let's handle it with kindness and love. Do not let things get out of hand where it can't be fixed and bitterness lingers.

We are the peace keepers. My mission is to bring about a Hotep Dynasty. The Hotep Dynasty is a family lineage of our people embracing their true identity, practicing our culture, living our truth and standing on righteousness.

Portion Six – War Zone

We are behind enemy lines. You are in a war right now. The tanks may not be rolling down the street at this moment but they're coming. All that I have instructed to you is for preparation of this time.

The black man, woman and child; the most hated people on the face of the planet. You may not believe this fact but there are so many documents and ways to prove this. We can go back to the Civil Rights Era and slavery. Black people were looked at as sub-human. We were looked at as beneath animals.

We see in the news every day how a black person has been killed with no real consequences for those that do the killing. We know for a fact of the experiments black people have been and are still being subjugated to. We know for a fact that drugs were pushed into our communities to destroy us.

Black people who were known as revolutionaries, have died fighting for the betterment of our people. Revolutionaries spoke out of the injustice and have exposed those who practiced injustice, not only on our people but the world over.

It seems like we as black people are against all odds. The system has been designed to keep us dumb downed. The media portrays the black man as a monster, a threat and a burden.

Destroy the image of a people then as you seek out to destroy them physically, no one will blink an eye. We are under the spell and program that the so called elite has been running.

Everybody is saying that these are the end times that we are living in right now. I know religious people have been saying this but also others. Those who study metaphysics have said this too. They are referencing the age in which we are living and how this is the age of information and transformation.

The Earth is changing. Earth has been described as a living entity vibrating on the third dimension and recently moved or is now moving to the fifth dimension. We as humans, when we get sick and catch colds from bacteria and viruses, the body raises its temperature to kill off the bad guys. The Earth is doing the same so you hear a lot of talk about global warming and how the Earth is getting hotter.

There are so many things we must prepare for. This isn't to scare you, this is to have you ready mentally and physically so that when things begin to occur, you can face them and act accordingly without losing focus and hope.

Remember that no matter the situation, you're going to always need: food, water and shelter. This is why you must learn how to farm. For the ones who still eat meat from time to time, this is why you must learn how to hunt. You must be able to grow your own food or have some type of food supply handy because running down to the local grocery store will not be an option during difficult times.

You must have a source of water. Living in rural areas or what is considered as the country has a benefit because you have your own well which runs in the ground and brings up your water. It's ran by an electric pump but with some modifications you can replace the electric pump with an old fashioned pitcher pump.

Being near or having access to a water source such as rivers and lakes are great too. These sources can be easily purified by boiling or either some type of purifier that can be placed into the water that is gathered in containers.

You may have a roof over your head but in the event that there's no power to your shelter, you must learn how to keep warm during cold months. Lots of blankets and extra clothing will come in handy. Fire starting skills are definitely needed. If some foods are to be cooked, how will you prepare it? These things must be thought of way beforehand.

Portion Seven – Man Up

I don't believe I should have to wait till my son turns 18 before I can consider him as a man. I believe in training him young. By the age of 13 my son should know what it takes to become a man and act as one from then on out.

It is my duty to prepare you for what is coming up ahead. You must be strong. You must be strong in spirit and in mind. Your purpose is to continue the Dynasty that I have begun. My purpose is to reset the minds and erase all programming that is detrimental to our people. It is my purpose to lay the foundation so that you may build upon it.

It's going to be a lot of things coming at you my son. Living in this world it seems like the people who try to live a righteous life have it the hardest. Many people would rather see evil prevail. We are the restorers of balance. We must make sure that good prevails because evil has been ruling for far too long.

You will be up against some of your own family and friends but you must continue to stay true to your mission and purpose. The world is ruled by evil people; you cannot go with the flow. You must rebel against the evil system that exists. Many people will think you're crazy because you will be aware of certain things that they are not. Do not be discourage. The knowledge that you have attained must be giving to those ready to receive it.

Stand on your truth. Read, study and research. Do not let your emotions and opinions rule over logic, rational thinking and facts. The human brain and mind are powerful. We have yet to tap into their full potential.

Since the world wants you to view yourself and others like you as a slave and a subhuman, I say to you my son, view yourself as a God. View yourself as someone who can create the good life that you deserve. View yourself as someone who can overcome any adversity. You are one with nature and you are highly favored when it comes to nature. Remain natural. Do what's natural. Everything that is normal isn't natural but everything that is natural is normal.

Do not get distracted by the media. That's a brainwashing medium. Look how we are depicted in the movies, television shows and radio. This is the image that is being broadcasted to other cities, states and countries in the world. This is why it is up to you to shed a different light on the matter. You must shed the true light. A righteous light. A pure light.

The wicked people that are ruling this planet right now hate to see a strong black man. They want you to be weak and feminine, so that they can control you. Be a man. Be strong. You must destroy what they have built. You must build what they have destroyed.

You are a man now my son. It is time for you to build your legacy. What will you offer the world that they may know you by when you leave?

Portion Eight – Full Circle

My son, may you be protected by the spirits of the ancestors and Heru. Heru represents a higher consciousness and rising above evil. Every day it's a battle between doing good and doing evil. Always choose good.

This path is far from easy although it should be. Spread your wings of righteousness and soar above the wicked. See that these people are beneath you and this is why they try to pull you down. You came from greatness and your ancestors have left instructions on how to return to that greatness. I am leaving you instruction on how to return to that greatness. You must also do your part.

As a child you should enjoy your youth and have fun. You should listen to the elders before you and gather the wisdom that they have attain throughout the many years they have walked on this earth.

Be mindful. Be respectful. When you have come upon your teenage years, you are now becoming a man. Soon you will have to put away all childish things. You may even have to sacrifice some of your childhood years for the greater good of your people's condition.

This is your rites of passage. I'm passing on to you, rituals in which you must partake to become a man in order for you to help your people, our people. I can't hold your hand and walk with you. I must point you to the way. I can show you the door but only you can walk through it.

Remember my son, you must first get your mind, body and spirit right. How do you do this? By learning as much about your history as possible. Learn about our people. Learn the diverse culture of our people. Take heed to the culture I bring before you. Study and research often. Read books regularly.

Eating right is important. Do not let your taste buds be perverted by chemicals and nonfood items. Fruits, vegetables and grains are the main foods to consume. Temptation will be inevitable especially if you are surrounded by people who do not wish to learn about their body and what is good or bad for them.

Getting the proper exercise is a must. We're getting too lazy as a people. When I was child I remembered seeing one or two people that may have been over weight. Now it seems like the reverse and only one or two people, even children, are slim or the proper weight.

I hope that I can spend more time outside myself but now I'm scated behind a computer handling business and typing up documents to create books for you. This is the sacrifice I'm making because I know it is worth it. I ask that you do not let my sacrifice be in vain.

So get outside, read a book under a tree or ride a bike. Meditate some and clear your mind. Answers to some of your questions can be found that way.

Once you have gotten the proper mind set and have conditioned the body with physical activities, you want to be able to support yourself financially. If you are still in America and the dollar is still the currency America uses, you'll have to acquire some to do business here.

This is where your gift, trade or skills come in. You'll have to have some type of resources to support yourself and later your family. Remember to keep in mind about the bartering system because this is what everything may revert to when the dollar is no longer the currency of choice in America and other countries. If you can purchase real gold and silver, then do so. Gold and silver are the real money.

You are now ready to take on a wife. Your queen. Find you a woman that you can build with. Let her be of great substance. She must be a woman who overstands her history and place in America and also your life. Teach her and guide her. Be her protector as she is your nurturer. Together you set goals and achieve them. You learn from one another. You help one another. You're able to talk to one another about everything. Do not put another woman before her or let any other woman come in between what you have.

With that woman you will build a solid family. Have children. Have as many as you see fit and able to care for properly. Teach your children their history and culture. Raise them up righteously.

It's also necessary that you are familiar with the laws of the land. A lot of our people are incarcerated and lose their freedom because we don't overstand how the court system works. It's not designed for us to win to begin with but I feel like if we learn these laws, regulations, statutes and codes that affect us, then we'll have a better chance of liberating ourselves in the court systems of the oppressors. By all means, avoid any type of run ins with police officers. Too many of our people are being killed by the hands of cops. Again I will repeat this, avoid any type of run ins with policy enforcers. I'm telling you to live your life and do what you must do but please do not knowingly commit some type of crime to give them reasons to harass you.

Once you have a solid family and overstanding of laws, you can then reach out to other likeminded individuals or groups. There's power in numbers and unity is very important. So many goals can be accomplished much quicker with the help of a community. You should be a self-sustainable community. In a self-sustainable community, everybody's helping out and doing the best they can to uplift the entire community.

Farming and bartering should play a big part in communities that are self-sustained. This is how you begin to heal our people. This is how you help our people. It all begins with your mind state. Your rites of passage will be like a ripple effect. It begins in the center and spreads out. You are of age now. Be a man.

If I'm not able to speak these words to you face to face, if I'm not able to teach you in the physical, then please accept this book in my absence. This is my peace offering. This is my Hotep.

Neter Ankh Hotep-El
(Divine Life of Peace)

www.ingramcontent.com/pod-product-compliance
Lightning Source LLC
Chambersburg PA
CBHW071734020426
42331CB00008B/2025